T0381972

The Butterfly Spotter's Guide

The Butterfly Spotter's Guide

MATTHEW OATES

Illustrated by
Ella Sienna

 National Trust

Published by National Trust Books
An imprint of HarperCollins Publishers,
1 London Bridge Street
London SE1 9GF
www.harpercollins.co.uk

HarperCollins Publishers,
Macken House,
39/40 Mayor Street Upper,
Dublin 1, D01 C9W8, Ireland

First published 2025
© National Trust Books 2025
Text © Matthew Oates
Illustrations © Ella Sienna

ISBN 978-0-00-871595-3
10 9 8 7 6 5 4 3 2 1

The contents of this publication are believed correct at the time of printing. Nevertheless,
the publisher can accept no responsibility for errors or omissions, changes in the detail
given or for any expense or loss thereby caused.

A catalogue record for this book is available from the British Library.

Printed and bound in India

If you would like to comment on any aspect of this book, please contact us at the above
address or national.trust@harpercollins.co.uk

National Trust publications are available at National Trust shops or online at
nationaltrustbooks.co.uk

This book is produced from independently certified FSC™ paper to ensure responsible
forest management.

For more information visit: www.harpercollins.co.uk/green

Contents

Introduction

Welcome to the wonderland that is butterflying. You will never stop learning, for however much we know about butterflies, there is always much more to discover.

Butterflies fascinate. We love them. To many of us, they are wandering magicians, clothed in colours that dazzle or impress. They arouse our curiosity and captivate. Be careful, they're addictive – and their caterpillars too. They are also in vogue, big time.

Butterflies are all around us, more so today as images than in actuality – look at the frequency of butterfly images in advertising, fashion, on TV and even as body tattoos. Sadly, around 80 per cent of British butterflies have declined over the last 50 or so years, and we must now travel to nature reserves and other protected places to see many species.

Fewer and fewer butterflies visit the places we inhabit, yet butterflies have long been one of the most popular elements of British wildlife. During Victorian and Edwardian periods, and for a while after, butterfly collecting was an immensely popular hobby. Today, photography has thankfully replaced the net and the fashion for displaying them in cabinets.

Beginners may be surprised how small most butterflies are – around the size of a 50 pence piece or a postage stamp. Only a few stand-out proudly at a distance, notably the golden male Brimstone, which can be spotted at distances of 70 metres.

Essentially, butterflies are changelings. They are insects that respond rapidly to environmental change – today, primarily to habitat loss – and increasingly to climate change. Many of their breeding places jump in and out of suitability; it might be right one year but not necessarily the next. Their status and distribution, though, have never been stable: there has always been radical change, with some species increasing spectacularly whilst others were declining. Even during the Victorian and Edwardian heyday, three species became extinct in Britain.

They are insects, and insects are seriously ambitious – they push limits, seeking pastures new: they want to take over the world. When it comes to personal ambition, nothing rivals a caterpillar. They have serious aspirations; they're going to fly!

Recently, a minor cultural revolution has taken place: butterflies have become cool. The move from collecting to photography has helped, and butterflying has piggybacked on the popularity of birding. Butterflies – magnificent and awe-inspiring as they are – make us feel happy; we humans are hard-wired to beauty, particularly natural beauty, and to wonder.

Butterflies are as essential to our experience of warm sunlit hours as birdsong is to a May morning. Better still, our scarcer species (and most of them are scarce) take us to the heart of our most treasured landscapes when those rare places are at the zenith of their annual cycle of natural beauty, and when the weather is fine. Butterflies are jewels on nature's crown.

Butterflies tell us a lot about the health of our environment, not least because they are well monitored through the UK Butterfly Monitoring Scheme (UKBMS). Consequently, they have been adopted by the government as official indicators of environmental health, along with the likes of farmland birds.

In scientific terms, the butterfly is the mature reproductive stage of a complex metamorphosis, the culmination of an incredible journey through the egg, caterpillar (or larval) and pupal (or chrysalis) stages. It would be a little wrong, though, to state that being a butterfly is all about reproduction. The adult butterfly is also the insect's dispersal stage, where it spreads to new habitats – eggs, caterpillars and pupae can't fly or form new colonies.

Butterflies are grouped into different families and are given English and scientific names (mostly Latin or classical Greek). Taxonomic fashion, though, periodically changes, so the families, scientific names, English names, and even the order of species, are subject to sudden changes. However, butterfly enthusiasts tend to love and retain the names they first learn.

There are currently five major families of British butterflies: Skippers (small brown or orange butterflies that supposedly skip along in flight); Whites and Yellows (a distinctive group of white or yellow-based butterflies); Browns, Fritillaries and Aristocrats (a large and varied family, of sizeable and often boldly marked butterflies); Metalmarks (a large and varied family of small to medium-sized butterflies globally, but with just one British and European representative, the Duke of Burgundy); Coppers, Hairstreaks and Blues (small, usually bright butterflies sharing the same distinctive wing shape).

There are 13 families of larger moths, and 42 families of micro moths – some 2,500 species in all! We have around 60 species of larger moth that fly readily by day, though few of them fly as purposefully as butterflies – if it seems to be directionless and crash-lands randomly, it's probably a moth.

Butterfly spotting is a great adventure, beset by initial challenges that you will soon overcome and eventually forget. The secret is never to make the same mistake twice.

Butterfly Must-knows

Butterfly or moth?
If butterflies are the wild orchids, moths are the
garden flowers – and they vastly outnumber their
cousins. The difference between butterflies and
moths is rather ambiguous. There are day-flying
moths, and some butterflies fly on warm moonlit
nights. The main difference is in the antennae,
which are clubbed or hooked in butterflies and thin
or feathery in moths. By day, though, butterflies
are far more direct and purposeful. Very few moths
settle with their wings folded upright above the body.
That's a strong butterfly characteristic.

Habitats

Some of our species of butterfly are habitat
specialists, restricted to specific habitats where their
caterpillar foodplant grows – and they may breed
only on a single species of plant. It's their habitats
that are rare: the butterflies themselves may abound
within these places. Other species are habitat
generalists, occupying a variety of places in which

their needs are met, and often using a range of larval (caterpillar) foodplants.

Many of our scarcer species seldom wander and are sedentary. Conversely, many of our more widespread species wander far and wide, whilst migrants such as the Painted Lady and Clouded Yellow may travel hundreds of miles to reach our shores. Much, though, depends on prevailing weather conditions – butterflies can spread extensively during long hot summers.

Our less mobile, more sedentary species must have all their habitat needs met in one place. The difficulty here is that places change, with suitable conditions rarely persisting for long, forcing the butterflies to move on, in search of new areas in which to breed. As our landscapes become more modified, to meet increasing human demands, so there are fewer places in which butterflies can breed.

Several of our rarer butterflies are so scarce and so restricted in their distribution that they are not included in this book. Leave the likes of the Black Hairstreak, Large Blue, Swallowtail and Wood White until you are familiar with the more common species. Some only appear in ultra-special summers: for example, something amazingly golden hurtling frenetically along the bottom of a south-facing slope is probably a Clouded Yellow, a migrant from the Mediterranean that occasionally comes here in numbers.

Lifespans

Most individual butterflies live for just a few days, especially the smaller ones – and many of ours are little bigger than thumbnail size. Larger butterflies may live for 10–15 days. We know this from scientific 'mark and recapture' studies, in which butterflies within a colony are netted, carefully marked on the wing undersides with fast-drying oil-based felt-tip pens, released, and later recaptured. This makes it possible to determine how long they live, how far they travel and, if we're lucky, to estimate population size.

However, six of our resident species spend the winter as hibernating butterflies, breeding in the spring. Individuals of these species can therefore live for seven or even 11 months (Comma, Peacock, Small Tortoiseshell, Large Tortoiseshell, Red Admiral and Brimstone). Most of our resident species overwinter as caterpillars, but nine spend the winter as eggs and eleven as pupae. A few species adopt more than one strategy.

Flight Seasons and Broods

The flight seasons of our 39 single-brooded species last five or six weeks, with individual butterflies emerging over a period of about three weeks during pulses of fine weather, not all at once. Occasionally – and increasingly – some of these species produce second-brood specimens in hot summers. The complication here is that some species are single-brooded in the north, but also further south during poor summers, yet are double-brooded down south during better summers. Climate change is altering the established patterns of seasonality, and butterfly flight seasons are occurring earlier and earlier.

Flight seasons usually start and end with low numbers, and have a distinct 'peak season' period when numbers are highest. Everything, though, depends on the weather – a spell of poor weather can end a flight season prematurely. Males dominate early on, females in the later stages.

Courtship and Mating

You might expect butterflies to indulge in sophisticated courtship rituals. A few do, but most courtship dances almost invariably end in male advances being rejected – indicating that the female was already mated. Some species, such as the White Admiral, indulge in elaborate follow-my-leader courtship flights. Mostly, though, it's a matter of getting in first.

Different species have different strategies for ensuring that boy meets girl early on in the female's life. Some males are territorial, occupying and defending sheltered vantage points against rival males, with virgin females gravitating into these territories. In other species, the males frenetically patrol for virgin females: for example, in the morning, Chalk Hill Blue males ceaselessly search areas of short turf where their foodplant (horseshoe vetch) grows, in order to mate with the newly emerged chocolate-brown females; Orange-tip males, however, wander up and down a stretch of sunny lane, intercepting anything dressed in white, in the hope that it's an available female.

For many species, the females mate just the once, either on the day of emergence or the next day. Mating itself typically lasts between 30 and 90 minutes. Thereafter, females tend to avoid males, as the males will want to mate many times. The females have to get on with the all-important job of laying eggs to ensure the next generation and don't want male interference with this.

This Book

This book is an introduction to British butterflies and day-flying moths, concentrating on species that people are most likely to see. It aims to get you started on a wonder-filled journey of lifelong discovery. A few of our rarer butterflies are excluded, as they are restricted to highly localised areas – specific nature reserves mainly. Two separate views (wings open and wings closed) have been included when it helps the reader to identify a specific butterfly. When the second view is of a female butterfly it has been noted in the text. You'll never stop learning about butterflies: there are no experts, as butterflies are so incredibly complex and ever-changing – and moths are considerably more numerous and far less well understood. Keep your L-plates proudly on!

Dingy Skipper

Erynnis tages

Physically, this dull, mottled grey-brown insect looks like a moth, but in character it's a butterfly – sun-loving, vibrantly active and impressively agile in flight. The males are as aggressive and inquisitive as the best of male butterflies. Behaviour alone separates them from the day-flying Burnet Companion moth, which suddenly crash-lands into the grasses in typical moth-like fashion.

Dingy Skippers fly for about six weeks during spring, close to the ground and at speed, though pausing to visit low-growing flowers or to bask. In poor weather they roost on dead flower heads, often those of the previous summer's common knapweed, with their wings folded around the flower head. The eggs are laid mainly on common bird's foot trefoil, though on limestone downs horseshoe vetch is also favoured. In hot summers, a few second-brood specimens emerge.

It lives in colonies, mainly on chalk downs and other limestone grasslands, but also in woodland rides and various other dry grasslands, including sand dunes.

I SPOTTED THIS BUTTERFLY

AT ....

ON ....

Small Skipper
and Essex Skipper

Thymelicus sylvestris and *T. lineola*

These two tiny, golden Skippers almost invariably inhabit the same rough grassland habitats, flying at the same time of year (late June into August) and living in colonies. The only sure way of separating them is to look at a settled specimen head-on through close-focusing binoculars: then, the undersides of the Essex Skipper's antennae appear to have been dipped in blackest ink, whilst those of its cousin are orange or dull brown. However, female Small Skippers often have dark-brown antennae, generating serious confusion. Additionally, the Small Skipper is strongly associated with the common and distinctive Yorkshire-fog grass – its females crawl backwards down the stems to tuck their eggs within the sheaths. Where that grass is abundant, Small Skippers are likely to dominate; where it's absent, any golden Skipper is more likely to be the Essex Skipper, which favours taller, coarse grasses. Both fly in southern rough grasslands.

I SPOTTED THIS BUTTERFLY

AT ....

ON ....

Large Skipper

Ochlodes sylvanus

The butterfly equivalent of the Harrier jump jet, specialising in rapid take-offs and whizzing around at impressive speeds in hot sunshine – the hotter the sun, the faster they fly, like a tiny orange fireball. The sparring males chase each other around spectacularly before a victor returns to a chosen territory. Both sexes often settle with forewings raised in a 'V' shape, whilst the hindwings are held horizontally. They visit a wide range of flowers, often favouring brambles.

This is a high-summer butterfly, flying from late May through to early August, peaking during midsummer. It's common in a wide variety of rough grassland habitats in lowland England, Wales and southern Scotland, especially favouring grassy woodland rides. It breeds on a variety of coarser grasses and smaller sedges.

I SPOTTED THIS BUTTERFLY

AT ....

ON ....

Orange-tip

Anthocharis cardamines

The males (opposite top), with their orange forewing splash, suggest a tropical butterfly – or something that has escaped from a butterfly house; yet this is one of our most widespread species, a quintessential part of springtime. The females (opposite bottom), however, lack the orange, and being shy and retiring become lost amongst the plethora of Small and Green-veined Whites – especially the latter, as they utilise many of the same foodplants.

Down south, Orange-tips fly from late March into early June, wandering incessantly as soon as the sun appears, favouring woods, lanes and damp meadows, and calm sunny weather. Further north, the flight season starts and ends later. There is only a single brood. In most districts, garlic mustard is the main foodplant, but cuckoo flower (lady's smock) and hedge mustard are commonly used, and honesty and dame's violet (sweet rocket) in gardens. Many larvae and overwintering pupae are destroyed during hedge and road-verge cutting.

I SPOTTED THIS BUTTERFLY

AT ....

ON ....

Large White and Small White

Pieris brassicae and *P. rapae*

Large and smaller variations of the same thing, although dwarf Large Whites are often seen, plus the occasional large Small White. Their larvae, though, are radically different: Large White larvae are yellow and black, and gregarious; Small White larvae are uniformly green, and loners. Both feed on a wide range of plants from the cabbage family, Cruciferae, wild and cultivated. In the wild, garlic mustard is very popular, as are the younger leaves of wild cabbage and sea-kale near the coast. In gardens, nasturtium and dame's violet are favoured – not just cabbages. Advice to gardeners: tightly net brassica crops except red cabbage, which they avoid. 'Cabbage Whites' fly throughout lowland Britain from April through to autumn, peaking between late July and early September. Sizeable immigrations take place in some years. The Southern Small White, which looks and behaves like a Small White but breeds on different plants (weeds mainly), is poised to colonise south-east England soon.

I SPOTTED THIS BUTTERFLY

AT ....

ON ....

Green-veined White

Pieris napi

The common and widespread Green-veined White is similar in size, shape and colouring to the Small White. Separating them is difficult. The thickened veins on the hindwing undersides seldom appear green, rather they are thickly suffused with grey scales on a yellowy background. The females are more distinctive, with prominent dull black blotches on their forewing upper sides and thickened, grey upper-side veining.

They fly during April and May, and again in July and August, with some third-brood specimens during September. In flight, the spring-brood males appear to have distinctly pointed forewings, achieved by how they angle their wings. Summer-brood specimens, though, seem rounder winged, and are less easy to distinguish from the Small White.

It does not breed on cabbages, but on a variety of mostly wild cruciferous plants – notably, garlic mustard, cuckoo flower and, oddly, watercress and wild horse radish. It's one of the most common butterflies in Scotland.

I SPOTTED THIS BUTTERFLY

AT ....

ON ....

Brimstone

Gonepteryx rhamni

An old saying claims that if your first butterfly of the year is a golden male Brimstone you will have a happy summer. On the first day of spring, the males emerge from hibernation and begin their wanderings – searching for the paler, lemony-green females. The original 'butter-coloured fly' is one of our easiest butterflies to identify. They get everywhere and are often seen stopping to feed from spring flowers.

The Brimstone breeds on buckthorn bushes, of which we have two native species (plus some garden cultivars). Eggs laid in spring produce a brood that emerges during July. These pristine butterflies feed up for a while, prior to hibernating for six or seven months in bramble tangles, ivy clumps and dense grass tussocks. In gardens, during August, they favour runner bean and perennial sweet pea flowers. The Brimstone is widespread in nearly all of England and Wales, and is spreading steadily north.

I SPOTTED THIS BUTTERFLY

AT ....

ON ....

How to Spot Butterflies

———————

Butterflies take us by surprise, appearing at varying speeds and distances, and looking different in different light and angles. Often, they're blink-and-miss-it experiences.

Their identification can take years to master. Worse still, they seem to become smaller as our eyesight deteriorates with age. Close-focusing binoculars are a huge help, although it takes time to become skilled at using them on small, fast-moving objects. Remember to raise the binoculars to your eyes whilst keeping your sight focused on the subject.

For the scarcer species, we have to travel to special places, mainly nature reserves – and be there in suitable weather conditions and at the right time of year. All the necessary information is readily available in books and on websites.

Each species can appear in myriad guises, depending on whether individuals are freshly emerged or old, faded and battered. Their wing scales rub off as they age, dulling their colours and hues. You need to learn all these different permutations – but don't worry, it will come. Try to guess the identity of every butterfly you see, wherever, however and whenever.

Tips:

- Concentrate on the easier species at first, such as the Marbled White and Peacock. Feel free to group the Large, Green-veined and Small Whites together, as 'Cabbage Whites', and the Small and Essex Skippers as 'Golden Skippers'.
- Concentrate on the showier, easier-to-identify males – leaving until later the difficult brown females of the Blues.
- Learn the habitats, foodplants and flight seasons.

Wall Brown

Lasiommata megera

A sizeable orange butterfly with black markings and rounded wings settling warily on bare ground, often along sunny footpaths and trackways, is likely to be this butterfly – especially if it plays follow-my-leader and flies on in front of you, only to resettle again and again. However, away from coastal habitats, it's quite a scarce butterfly these days, having mysteriously declined inland since the mid-1980s.

It has two broods, the first in early summer, then a second, usually stronger, brood during late July and August. There is a partial third brood in early autumn, after hot summers. The males squabble like mad.

Eggs are mostly laid on grass rootlets along eroded bank overhangs, old tractor ruts, or in the ceilings of rabbit holes. The young larvae feed on fine, needlelike grasses, before moving onto coarser grasses as they develop. They move back to the overhangs to pupate.

I SPOTTED THIS BUTTERFLY

AT ....

ON ....

Speckled Wood

Pararge aegeria

A dark but distinctive butterfly with cream spots. The males establish and defend sunspot territories along shady woodland paths. When two meet up, they squabble terribly – often for several minutes, before a victor emerges. No other British butterfly disputes the ownership of a shaft of light along overhung woodland paths like the Speckled Wood. The males change territories as sunspots come and go, as the sun moves around. The slightly larger and paler females are somewhat shy and retiring, though they will readily disperse over treeless ground, out in the open.

The eggs are laid on soft grasses in dappled shade, favouring the distinctive light-green false brome-grass. The butterflies fly from late March or early April (in the far south) through to mid-autumn, being continuously brooded. They have been seen in every month of the year in the far south west. This is a good-news butterfly, which has spread throughout most of the UK in recent decades, living in a variety of habitats, including gardens.

I SPOTTED THIS BUTTERFLY

AT

ON

Small Heath

Coenonympha pamphilus

This is one of our most widespread butterflies,
inhabiting dry grasslands throughout the UK, up
to about 600 metres on mountainsides. However,
it's one of our eight butterfly species that settle only
with their wings tightly closed, above their bodies,
so you can never admire the goldy-brown upper
sides, just the drab brown and grey-flushed-with-
pink undersides. It's also one of our smallest
butterflies – about the size of a thumbnail – so we
tend to overlook it. On the wing from early May
through to mid-September, with brood peaks during
June and August.

The Small Heath is at its loveliest when feasting on
carpets of carmine-pink wild thyme on midsummer
days. It has the habit of turning up in precisely the
same spot, such as a sheltered dell, year on year. The
males are feisty, sparring with each other and taking
on much larger winged insects that invade their
chosen spot.

I SPOTTED THIS BUTTERFLY

AT ....

ON ....

Scotch Argus

Erebia aethiops

Widespread and locally abundant in the lightly grazed parts of the hilly regions of Scotland, breeding on a variety of grasses, especially the abundant purple moor-grass. Some colonies are huge, extending over extensive tracts of hillsides. It is, though, rare or absent on hills heavily grazed by sheep. In England, there are isolated stations in Cumbria – along the old railway line at Smardale, and on Arnside Knott – and the butterfly has a diffuse presence in Upper Wharfedale in North Yorkshire.

This is very much an August butterfly, the Meadow Brown of the far north. It's relatively large and distinctive – jet black with prominent reddish spots when freshly emerged, though the black fades to brown with age. It can be confused only with the smaller and browner Mountain Ringlet, which blows about on the Lake District mountains and in the south-west Highlands during midsummer, mainly above the 500-metre contour.

I SPOTTED THIS BUTTERFLY

AT ....

ON ....

Ringlet

Aphantopus hyperantus

The Ringlet can be confused with a male Meadow
Brown, but it's jet black when freshly emerged
and it flies differently – in flight, Meadow Browns
bib-bob, Ringlets jerk. The two species are easily
separated when they fly together in rough grasslands,
during late June to early August. Crucially, the
Ringlet's golden rings, infilled with black and
pupilled with white, are distinctive and diagnostic.
When freshly emerged, it has an iridescent sheen
on its darkling wings.

Ringlets occur in colonies in dry and damp rough
grasslands and clay woodlands in much of England,
Wales, Scotland and Northern Ireland. The larvae
feed on a range of coarse grasses. The butterflies
will fly in dull weather, even in rain, if it's warm.
This, though, is one butterfly which fares poorly in
heatwaves, vanishing into deep shade and ending its
flight season early.

I SPOTTED THIS BUTTERFLY

AT ....

ON ....

Meadow Brown

Maniola jurtina

One of our most common and widespread butterflies, occurring in large colonies in nearly all lowland grassland habitats throughout the UK – with the notable exception of modern rye grass fields treated with artificial fertilisers or slurry. The larvae feed on grasses, other than agricultural rye grass.

It flies from early June (or even the end of May) right through to late September, and even into October or beyond. Numbers are highest during the mid-June to mid-July period, though there can be a second peak during August.

Freshly emerged specimens are surprisingly dark, but not as black as those of the Ringlet, though they fade with age and quieten down too. Very old specimens (maybe three weeks old) are pale brown. The females have a bright forewing splash that fades as they age. They all love flowers, jostling for position on plants such as knapweeds, thistles and brambles.

I SPOTTED THIS BUTTERFLY

AT ....

ON ....

Gatekeeper

Pyronia tithonus

In contrast to most of our butterfly species, the males of the Gatekeeper are extremely well behaved – never fighting, and showing polite consideration towards the females. It used to be called the Hedge Brown, rightly so as it's essentially a butterfly of hedges and scrub, though it will cluster away from scrub lines on clumps of favoured flowers, like wild marjoram.

It's much brighter than its cousin, the Meadow Brown, with a deep-orange base colour broken up and bordered by deep brown, and with a pair of white-pupilled eyespots in the forewings. The male has a broad dark band across the forewing upper side, whilst the female is far brighter.

It can be found in colonies in bushy places, flying from early July through to late August over much of lowland England and Wales. It's gradually spreading north, and does particularly well in hot summers.

I SPOTTED THIS BUTTERFLY

AT ....

ON ....

Marbled White

Melanargia galathea

Perhaps our easiest butterfly to identify, being our only piebald species. In continental Europe, though, there are several similar-looking species.

Here, it's primarily a butterfly of dry southern limestone grasslands, though it can be found as far north as the North Yorkshire Moors. It has been moving steadily north and has overspilled into rough acidic grasslands, dry and damp. It's most abundant on the southern chalk downs, in the Mendips and on the Cotswold commons.

Marbled Whites fly for about six weeks (as do many butterflies), from mid-June to early August, in colonies in rough grassland. They congregate on flowers such as knapweeds, marjoram, scabiouses and thistles. The larvae feed on grasses, favouring places where red fescue forms an underlayer beneath taller, coarser grasses.

In Greek mythology, Galatea was a beautiful nymph, mentioned in Ovid and Virgil, and celebrated in Handel's operatic masque *Acis and Galatea*.

I SPOTTED THIS BUTTERFLY

AT ....

ON ....

Photographing Butterflies

This wonderfully absorbing hobby has replaced old-fashioned collecting. It is challenging, however, as butterflies are seldom cooperative. You can use a good camera phone, or buy the best and lightest camera you can afford, and with the best lens – you won't enjoy lugging heavy equipment up a hillside. Please remember, the butterfly and its habitat come first. Tips for success:

- Pale sun on calm days with relatively low temperatures provide the best photography conditions. Butterflies tend to go hyper in warm sun and wobble about in windy weather.
- Some species hate being photographed, notably the Wall Brown! Others are relatively easy, such as the Gatekeeper.
- Females are easier than males, being more prone to sitting still.
- Watch your shadow. Be careful not to cast your shadow over a butterfly – you'll frighten it off.
- Concentrate on photographing feeding butterflies – watch the tongue. Those that are basking to warm up are easier, as are mating pairs.

Small Pearl-bordered Fritillary

Boloria selene

The Small Pearl-bordered Fritillary (opposite top) is one of two similar-looking species, the other being the much scarcer Pearl-bordered Fritillary (opposite bottom). The upper sides of both are hard to distinguish. This graceful butterfly occurs throughout western Britain, in bracken-filled combes, on heathy commons and hillsides, in grasslands on Carboniferous Limestone, on marshy bottoms, loch sides and, more rarely, in woodland clearings. It breeds on violets, favouring common dog violets under bracken and marsh violet in marshes. Most colonies fly during late May and June, but those in south-west England often start in late April and produce a smaller second brood during August. Separating the two 'pearl-bordereds' isn't easy. The central zone of the hindwing underside holds four silver splashes punctuated by dark brown splodges with prominent black spots. The female upper sides usually have an obvious pale border, which separates them instantly from the earlier-flying Pearl-bordered Fritillary. If it's flying after early June, it's a Small Pearl-bordered Fritillary.

I SPOTTED THIS BUTTERFLY

AT ....

ON ....

Silver-washed Fritillary

Argynnis paphia

This is the happiness butterfly – big, orange and
bouncy, the 'Tigger' of our butterfly fauna. It's the
largest of our fritillaries and the easiest to identify.
The female upper sides, though, are duller and paler
than those of the bright-orange males, and there is a
rare greeny-grey female colour form (known as form
valezina). The forewing tips are somewhat pointed and
there are no silver pearls on the hindwing undersides
– instead, the silver is mingled in with a green wash.

These giant butterflies fly from mid-June through
to late August, or even early September, in woodland
rides and clearings in southern England and Wales,
and also in the southern Lake District. They cluster
on bramble flowers, but spread out from the woods
when the brambles finish. This is another good-news
butterfly, which has been spreading steadily north
and east in recent decades. It breeds on common dog
violet clumps amongst leaf litter under trees.

I SPOTTED THIS BUTTERFLY

AT ....

ON ....

Dark Green Fritillary

Speyeria aglaja

A strong-flying orange-with-black butterfly of high-summer days, occupying a variety of habitats throughout almost all of the UK: chalk and limestone downs, sea combes, cliffs and sand dunes, heathy hillsides, bracken commons and loch sides. It is, though, surprisingly rare in woods.

Named after Aglaja, one of the three Graces in Greek mythology, the butterfly flies from mid-June through to early August – earlier in the south west, later in the far north (where the females are often heavily suffused with black). The adults love thistle and knapweed flowers. The butterfly breeds on violets, usually common dog violet or hairy violet, amongst grass tussocks.

It's very similar to the endangered High Brown Fritillary, which is sadly restricted to a few hillsides in Dartmoor, Exmoor, South Glamorgan and south Cumbria. The two often fly together – separating them out on the wing is almost impossible. The dark green on the hindwing undersides is punctuated by silver pearls.

I SPOTTED THIS BUTTERFLY

AT ....

ON ....

White Admiral

Limenitis camilla

Perhaps our most graceful butterfly in flight, cleverly and beauteously hugging the foliage contours of trees and bushes along woodland rides in midsummer, where it swoops and soars in search of its beloved bramble flowers. It's easily separated from the much-larger Purple Emperor, being our only black butterfly with prominent white bands, and much smaller and far less powerful and aggressive than the Emperor, and with well-rounded forewings. If in any doubt, it's a White Admiral, not an Emperor, though the two fly at the same time of year. The Admiral's wings soon get torn and tattered on the brambles.

The White Admiral is found in shady woods in southern England and south-east Wales, where it breeds on tangles of honeysuckle growing in dappled shade. The tiny larvae overwinter within a folded leaf, called a hibernaculum, feeding up and pupating during the spring.

I SPOTTED THIS BUTTERFLY

AT ....

ON ....

Purple Emperor

Apatura iris

Large, powerful and fearless, the Emperor is like no other British butterfly. It's essentially a canopy-dweller that lives diffusely over large tracts of southern wooded landscapes. It seldom visits flowers, favouring sap runs on oak or beech trees, and various unsavoury substances on woodland rides – including dog poo (though fox poo is greatly preferred). The males possess an iridescence that flashes in the ultra-UV range, through deep purple, myriad blues, into violet and beyond. However, we seldom see this. Mostly, they use it as a weapon against other males – or anything else that invades their treetop territories. The giant females skulk around sallow bushes on which the insect breeds – we mostly see them when they get flushed out by pestilent males. The Purple Emperor flies for five regal weeks during the midsummer period, and is expanding its range – or kingdom – dramatically, including into suburban green spaces and parks where sallows grow. Its Latin name is particularly apt: Iris, in Greek mythology, was the winged messenger of the gods, who appeared as a shimmering rainbow.

I SPOTTED THIS BUTTERFLY

AT ....

ON ....

Red Admiral

Vanessa atalanta

Until the start of the 21st century, the distinctive Red Admiral struggled to survive our winters, but it's increasingly managing to do so, as hibernating butterflies and as slow-growing larvae on patches of common nettle in frost-free hollows. Traditionally, it was primarily a migrant here, arriving in modest numbers in spring, breeding up rapidly, and becoming numerous in late summer and autumn. Most of these autumn beauties emigrate – they are spotted flying out to sea by south-coast birders; but those that emerge too late to migrate hunker down here for the winter, often in buildings, but sometimes in hollow trees and old rabbit burrows.

Consequently, the Red Admiral is now the first butterfly we tend to see in the year, and also the last – not least because it can fly in lower temperatures than other butterflies. It has overtaken the Small Tortoiseshell as our most familiar garden butterfly, feeding on flowers and fallen autumn fruits.

I SPOTTED THIS BUTTERFLY

AT ....

ON ....

Painted Lady

Vanessa cardui

Everything about the Painted Lady is special. This is a super migrant, often coming all the way from North Africa. Small influxes can arrive at any time of year, including during the winter. Most arrivals, though, take place during the late spring and early summer months. Sometimes, hundreds of thousands arrive – as in 1996, 2009 and 2013 – taking the British Isles by storm to produce a big home-grown brood, which then emigrates in early autumn. Occasionally, though, they fail to show up, as in the hot summer of 1984 and again in 2023.

Travel-worn migrants appear as pale-grey pilgrims, but home-grown specimens are splendidly coloured – our only pink-looking butterfly, quite unlike any other. Migrant males are stroppy and territorial, often gathering on hilltops in hope of finding a mate there. Conversely, the UK males tamely quaff nectar from flowers, before heading back south. It breeds mainly on thistles, defoliating them in years of abundance. Its Latin name, *cardui*, means 'of thistle'.

I SPOTTED THIS BUTTERFLY

AT ....

ON ....

Peacock

Aglais io

Easy to identify, this is our only butterfly with huge peacock eyes – similar to RAF roundels – on the wing upper sides. The undersides are completely black. In flight, this appears as a large dark butterfly with a distinct maroon tinge – the false eyes are only visible when the insect is basking.

Peacocks overwinter as hibernating butterflies, in wood piles, hollow trees and dark roof spaces. They mate and lay eggs in spring, exclusively on sunny common nettle patches. The shiny and spiny black caterpillars are gregarious, and quite distinctive. The new brood emerges during July – early in hot summers, later in wet ones – and feed up for a while on nectar prior to entering hibernation, unmated.

The Peacock is quite common in lowland Britain but is steadily moving north and may become double-brooded with climate change. A second brood can emerge in September during extremely hot summers, such as 1976 and 2018, and is commonplace in the Isles of Scilly.

I SPOTTED THIS BUTTERFLY

AT ....

ON ....

Small Tortoiseshell

Aglais urticae

The archetypal garden butterfly, often confused with
the larger and very differently marked Red Admiral.
The Small Tortoiseshell is a medium-sized butterfly
with, on the wing upper sides, areas of reddish-
orange punctuated by bold black markings, plus
yellow patches and distinctive blue pearls along the
outer edges. The undersides are mottled with black,
grey and buff.

This butterfly is found throughout lowland UK.
However, in recent decades, populations in the
south and east have plummeted – for reasons as yet
unknown. It overwinters as a butterfly, often in
garden sheds and in attics, emerging in early spring
to breed on common nettle patches in sunny, warm
situations. The new brood of pristine butterflies
emerges in late May or during June. This, in theory,
produces a new brood in late summer – but in recent
years, many June adults have gone into hibernation
instead. The goal posts are moving: this butterfly is
in rapid decline.

I SPOTTED THIS BUTTERFLY

AT ....

ON ....

Comma

Polygonia c-album

A distinctive butterfly – no other British butterfly has uniformly jagged wings. Also, it is far more tawny than any of the fritillaries, resembling the autumn leaves amongst which it may hibernate. The 'comma' refers to a C-shaped white mark on the hindwing undersides.

This is another good news story, for this butterfly has spread spectacularly over the last century. It now occurs throughout lowland England and Wales, and is now colonising Scotland and Northern Ireland. However, it's a loner, rarely seen with others. It breeds mainly on common nettles in dappled sunshine, but also strongly favours elms and wild hop.

This is one of six resident British butterflies that overwinter in the adult stage. In early spring, the butterflies pair up, the females then lay eggs that produce a much lighter-coloured brood from mid-June (called form *hutchinsoni*, named after an early entomologist). More, darker, butterflies emerge as summer fades into autumn. These then hibernate.

I SPOTTED THIS BUTTERFLY

AT ....

ON ....

Gardening for Butterflies

Every garden, even the smallest, can help butterflies. Although the two true Cabbage Whites will breed on nasturtiums planted in an apartment window box – even several floors up – it's very difficult to provide garden breeding conditions for most of our species.

Concentrate on growing nectar-rich flowers that butterflies favour. If you can, mow less: leave parts of your lawn rough. At the very least, plant a buddleia – the aptly-named butterfly bush. There are even dwarf buddleias, bred for patio containers. Other top butterfly nectar plants are asters/Michaelmas daisies (late summer and autumn flowering), aubrietia (spring), dame's violet (early summer), *Erysimum* 'Bowles's Mauve' (early summer), echinops (late summer), *Eupatorium* (late summer), marjoram (high summer) and *Verbena bonariensis* (late summer). However, many modern cultivars have had the scent and nectar bred out of them to make them flower longer. They attract few butterflies. Some classic butterfly nectar plants have fallen spectacularly from grace because of this, notably the once-popular ice plant *Sedum spectabile* (autumn) which has been replaced by nectarless hybrids that butterflies ignore.

Duke of Burgundy

Hamearis lucina

No one knows how 'His Grace' acquired this impressive name. The thumbnail-sized males are fiercely territorial, sparring together and taking on allcomers in favoured sheltered spots – for example, a sunken track or dell – which are occupied year after year. The females gravitate into those male lekking grounds (communal male displaying areas) on their maiden flights and are mated instantly, without so much as a by-your-leave. They then disperse, wisely. The males are especially resentful of the Dingy Skipper, a sun-loving dull-brown moth-mimic that is a fearsome rival.

   The Duke of Burgundy is the only British representative of the Metalmark family. Sadly, this is now a rare butterfly of sheltered rough grassland combes and slope bottoms on chalk and other limestones, where it breeds on cowslip, flying from mid-April into early June. Formerly, it was locally common in woods, breeding on cowslip and primrose, but it became an unscheduled victim of the 20th-century conifer revolution.

I SPOTTED THIS BUTTERFLY

AT ....

ON ....

Small Copper

Lycaena phlaeas

A fiery dart of a butterfly that is found in a variety of habitats throughout the British Isles, breeding on sorrel leaves growing among pockets of bare ground. It's most common on sandy heaths, acidic sand dunes and old-fashioned meadows on acidic soils, where it breeds on its favourite plant, sheep's sorrel. On neutral and calcareous soils, where it's primarily a butterfly of so-called 'wasteland', common sorrel is mainly used, and populations tend to be smaller.

Small Coppers fly in two or three broods from mid-April to early November, the second of which (in August) is almost invariably the strongest. The males are highly territorial, launching their tiny but wilful selves at anything invading their air space. It basks on bare ground.

It's a diminutive but utterly distinctive butterfly, being our only copper-coloured species (the much larger Large Copper, a vibrant flame, is long extinct).

I SPOTTED THIS BUTTERFLY

AT ....

ON ....

Purple Hairstreak

Favonius quercus

As the Latin name *quercus* suggests, this small butterfly is strongly associated with oaks, breeding on a wide range of these trees, native and non-native, including holm oak.

It's surprisingly common in lowland oak landscapes in England and Wales, though scarcer in Scotland and rare in Northern Ireland. In many southern districts, it's probably the most common high-summer butterfly. However, it is quiescent during the day, becoming active in early evening, when it does its courtship and mating, putting on spectacular evening flights along sheltered wood edges. Look for grey butterflies circle-dancing along west-facing oak edges on still, warm July evenings, from 6pm to 7.30pm. Take binoculars.

The purple iridescence is confined to the male upper sides; the females have only a purple forewing splash. It's seldom seen, except when freshly emerged specimens bask amongst grasses and bracken – incredibly, larvae descend to the ground to pupate. The undersides are uniformly grey.

I SPOTTED THIS BUTTERFLY

AT ....

ON ....

Green Hairstreak

Callophrys rubi

A beautiful but small and cryptic butterfly that flies throughout spring in a variety of sheltered habitats across almost all of the UK. It settles only with closed wings, which are emerald coloured (*rubi* here means 'of bramble', on which it sometimes breeds, rather than 'ruby'). The upper sides are a rich brown but only show in flight.

It occurs in loose colonies in a vast variety of habitats, breeding on a surprising diversity of plants. The strongest colonies breed on bilberry on moorland, cranberry in raised bogs, common rock rose on southern downs, and gorses on warm heathy slopes and sea cliffs. Colonies mainly inhabit sheltered places, such as combes. The males are territorial and aggressive.

The 'hairstreak' here is a line of white dots, often reduced to one or two, especially in downland colonies.

I SPOTTED THIS BUTTERFLY

AT ....

ON ....

The Inspiring Beauty of Butterflies

O ur love for butterflies runs deep. They are powerful symbols of beauty, freedom and personal achievement. They are massive in literature and poetry – writer and poet John Masefield called them 'the souls of summer hours'.

In art, they are associated mainly with freedom or death – and resurrection. Our fascination starts young, as demonstrated by the popularity of Eric Carle's book *The Very Hungry Caterpillar*. They are everywhere as symbols, from fashion to advertising. You are never far from a butterfly emblem.

Greek mythology held that when we die our souls depart on the wings of a butterfly (the Aztecs had similar beliefs). In ancient Greece, Psyche was the goddess of the human soul – hence psychology, psychotherapy and so on. Deeper still, psyche (with a small p) is the classical Greek word for butterfly. In Irish folklore, white butterflies represent the souls of lost children.

Holly Blue

Celastrina argiolus

The only blue butterfly that flits around bushes, and the commonest blue butterfly in gardens, parks and suburbia in general. It used to be called the Azure Blue: indeed, the males have bright azure upper sides, the paler females having dark forewing tips. There are no orange spots on the undersides, just small black dots on a blue-grey background – this separates it from all other Blues, except the scarce Small Blue and very rare Large Blue (which are not covered in this book). There are two broods, in spring and again in July and August, with occasional third-brood specimens down south. There are good Holly Blue years, and a great many poor years – due to the weather (it does well in sequences of hot summers), but also because its larvae can be heavily parasitised by the grubs of a tiny black-and-yellow wasp called *Listrodomus nycthemerus*. In spring, the larvae feed on the developing fruits of a wide range of shrubs, wild and cultivated – not just holly. The summer brood breeds primarily, and in many places exclusively, on ivy buds, flowers and berries.

I SPOTTED THIS BUTTERFLY

AT ....

ON ....

Silver-studded Blue

Plebejus argus

A petite bright-blue jewel of a butterfly (in the males) with lead (rather than silver) pearls and studs outside the orange zone on the hindwing undersides.

We have several subspecies, occupying different habitats and breeding on different plants, and varying a bit in size and colouring. We know it mainly as a heathland butterfly, inhabiting dry and wet heaths in southern England and in Wales, breeding mainly on young heathers in burnt, grazed or cut areas. However, colonies are also found on sand dune systems in south-west England and south-west Wales, breeding on common bird's foot trefoil, and there are limestone populations around Purbeck in Dorset and on and around the Great Orme in Conwy, where a dwarf race occurs in profusion in midsummer.

The males are a bright mid-blue, darkening around the wing edges. Most of the females are brown, but some races have dark-blue females. Look for courting or mating pairs.

I SPOTTED THIS BUTTERFLY

AT ....

ON ....

Brown Argus and Northern Brown Argus

Aricia agestis and *A. artaxerxes*

Southern and northern versions of a very small dark-brown butterfly with some orange spotting on the upper side edges, especially in the females. They are readily confused with female Common Blues, but the males of both these two species are aggressive. If you see a miniscule brown thug attacking another butterfly, it's a male Brown Argus or Northern Brown Argus. The placid females can indeed be confused with Common Blue females.

The Brown Argus, down south, has two broods, during May and early June, and again from mid-July to early September. It inhabits downland, calcareous sand dunes and other grasslands, breeding on common rock rose on chalky soils and, increasingly, on small annual cranesbills in other dry lowland habitats – including arable field edges.

The Northern Brown Argus is confined to calcareous grassland in northern England and Scotland, flying during July. It breeds only on rock roses. There is often a white spot in the forewing upper side.

I SPOTTED THIS BUTTERFLY

AT ....

ON ....

Common Blue

Polyommatus icarus

Our commonest blue butterfly, living in loose colonies in most grassland habitats throughout the UK – with the notable exception of fertilised rye grass fields.

The males (opposite top) have bright blue upper sides with white wing edges unbroken by blackened veins (though these white borders wear away in time), and uniformly grey undersides with black spots and orange hindwing markings. The females (opposite bottom) are either deep blue or dull brown, but always with orange spots on the hindwing upper-side edges; their undersides are brownish, with black spots and orange marginal markings. See also Adonis Blue and Brown Argus.

It breeds on common and greater bird's foot trefoils and clovers, usually amongst short turf or in bare ground pockets for warmth. Double-brooded down south, flying in May and June and again from late July into September, but usually single-brooded, during midsummer, up north and in woods. Can quickly form large colonies in modern herbal ley fields, containing its favoured trefoils, clovers and lucerne.

I SPOTTED THIS BUTTERFLY

AT

ON

Chalk Hill Blue

Polyommatus coridon

The commonest of our two specialist Blues of
southern limestone hills, the other being its cousin,
the Adonis Blue (see overleaf). The two species are
of the same size – quite large for a Blue – and share
the same larval foodplant: horseshoe vetch. Both
can occur in profusion. Both also have chocolate
brown females (opposite bottom), which are hard
to separate. However, the male Chalk Hill (opposite
top) is distinctive, wearing a light and almost
iridescent Cambridge blue, unique amongst our
butterflies. The females are easiest to spot when
observing mating pairs.

By and large, the Chalk Hill favours slightly longer
turf than its cousin, so hillsides only support strong
colonies of both species if horseshoe vetch grows
in areas of both short- and medium-height turf.
In some districts, notably Dorset, the Chalk Hill is
in decline, whilst the Adonis is in ascendancy – we
don't yet know why. Chalk Hill colonies are single-
brooded, flying from mid-July through to early
September on downland slopes.

I SPOTTED THIS BUTTERFLY

AT ....

ON ....

Adonis Blue

Polyommatus bellargus

This was a rare butterfly during the late 20th century, but its fortunes have been revived by conservation efforts, which have restored essential grazing to neglected south-facing downland slopes. It's double-brooded, with a mid-May to late-June brood and then a late-summer brood which is usually more profuse. Colonies now occur in the Cotswolds and on the chalk downs of southern England.

Adonis males are mid-blue, but with a stunning electric sheen – far brighter and more iridescent than Common Blue males. Also, Adonis males (and females) have prominent black vein ends that extend through the white wing-edge borders, and show on both the upper and undersides. However, the females are extremely challenging to identify. It takes years to learn how to separate old, worn females of the Adonis and Chalk Hill in late summer. Look for the scatter of blue wing scales close to the body. If they're electric blue it's an Adonis. If they're light blue it's a Chalk Hill.

I SPOTTED THIS BUTTERFLY

AT ....

ON ....

The Butterflying Scene

Butterflies have long been one of the most popular elements of British wildlife. Today, they are probably the second most popular group amongst wildlife enthusiasts after birds – not bad considering that we only have about 60 resident species, plus a few rare vagrants. Many birders are now going butterflying, as they can use binoculars effectively and aren't doing much birding during the high-summer months. Butterflying takes you to some of the most wonderful and special places in our islands. It's almost impossible to be bored when butterflying – too much is happening.

Most enthusiasts get into butterflies during their twenties; those who develop an interest as children tend to lose it during their teens but then return to it later.

The butterflying scene is at its brightest within the local branches of Butterfly Conservation. Becoming an active member of one of these is the best way to develop helpful knowledge, and to contribute to the conservation, surveying and monitoring of butterflies and moths. A massive welcome awaits you.

Hummingbird Hawkmoth

Macroglossum stellatarum

The Hummingbird Hawkmoth is the first of five day-flying moths featured in this book to help distinguish moths from butterflies. It's a large and most aptly named moth, which readily flies by day, hovering distinctively whilst sipping nectar from tall flowers through a long, probing tongue. Its grey-and-orange wings beat so frenetically that they become almost invisible, giving the impression of a large, hovering grey-and-white bullet – which suddenly whizzes off.

This is a good-news insect, as it seems to be colonising southern Britain, as our flora and fauna adapt to climate change (warmer winters, in particular). Formerly, it was an infrequent migrant, straying here in hotter summers. It abounded during the hot summer of 2022.

The moth breeds on bedstraws, favouring yellow lady's bedstraw growing in hotspots. It's strongly attracted to gardens, where it feeds from a variety of flowers, especially buddleias.

I SPOTTED THIS MOTH

AT ....

ON ....

Mint Moth

Pyrausta aurata

Also known as the Small Purple and Gold, and with a close cousin, *Pyrausta purpuralis*. This is a tiny moth with a distinctive gold spot in its purple forewings, and black-and-yellow-striped undersides. Once you've spotted it and realised how small it is, you will see many more, for it tends to live in loose colonies, often in gardens, where it's becoming increasingly common.

It flies in two broods, during early and late summer. The miniscule, dull caterpillars feed on mints, catmint, calamint, marjorams and thymes, including garden cultivars. Its darker cousin breeds primarily on thyme.

Mint moths are champions of our micro-moth fauna, a huge, fascinating and varied group of mainly tiny moths that are becoming more and more popular. 'Micros' are difficult to learn, but new identification books are paving the way, and Mint moths are portal species – leading you into a brave new world of mothing.

I SPOTTED THIS MOTH

AT ....

ON ....

Burnet Moths

Zygaena spp.

Several types of Burnet moth are found in Britain, though some are rare. They are oddly shaped day-flying moths, with thick black bodies that are distinctive in flight, and unusually narrow red-and-black wings. They are distinctive as Burnet moths, though separating them out into species is hard.

Three species are relatively common: the Five-spot Burnet, the Narrow-bordered Five-spot Burnet and the Six-spot Burnet. However, the spots are not easy to count or differentiate, and the borders are narrow anyway, and two species may fly together. All three have five or six large red spots on their otherwise coal-black forewings, and red hindwings with narrow black borders. They fly from late May to early August.

Burnet moths are found mainly in dry grasslands, where they breed on common bird's foot trefoil and, sometimes, other vetches. Populations are particularly strong on downland and other calcareous grasslands. Children love finding the straw-coloured cocoons fixed high on sturdy dead stems.

I SPOTTED THIS MOTH

AT ....

ON ....

Cinnabar

Tyria jacobaeae

Unmistakable, boldly clad in scarlet and black, differing distinctively from the Burnet moths, which have thickset antennae and very fat bodies. The Cinnabar is more butterfly-like.

The familiar black-and-yellow-striped 'rugby jersey' larvae are an essential part of childhood. They are commonly found defoliating ragwort plants, leaving just the bare stems – indeed, at times they play a significant role in controlling this so-called weed, eating out entire ragwort colonies and practising biological control.

The moth flies from mid-spring through to late summer, in loose colonies. The larvae feed on ragworts and groundsels, in high to late summer, before pupating just under the soil surface – the pupae are commonly dug up by gardeners.

This is primarily a moth of dry, rabbit-grazed grasslands, disturbed ground (including allotments) and, especially, sand dunes where common ragwort is a natural component.

I SPOTTED THIS MOTH

AT ....

ON ....

Silver Y

Autographa gamma

The archetypal moth: largely grey and medium-sized, which we flush up whilst walking through long grass, only for it to career off a few metres before randomly crash landing. It's primarily a migrant, venturing here in variable numbers each summer, quickly producing home-grown broods from a variety of low-growing plants, wild and cultivated.

Crucially, Silver Ys come here in vast numbers during summers that are good for other migrant moths, butterflies and other migratory winged insects, such as dragonflies and hoverflies. This makes it an important indicator species – look out for other migrants when the Silver Ys are numerous. It is best seen when freshly emerged adults are hovering in front of garden flowers, such as buddleias, quaffing nectar. The silver 'Y' marking on the forewing is quite distinctive – if you can get close enough to the moth to see it, and if the specimen is in good condition (migrant specimens tend to be very worn from travelling so far).

I SPOTTED THIS MOTH

AT ....

ON ....

Glossary

Broods Individual generations of butterflies are called broods. Most of our butterflies have a single brood, or generation, each year, but several have two broods (usually a first brood in spring or early summer and a second brood in late summer), and a few will have three or even more broods annually.

> **Single brood** Species such as Marbled White, Silver-washed Fritillary and Chalk Hill Blue are single-brooded, producing just one generation of adult butterflies each year.

> **First brood** The spring or early summer generation of a species which produces more than one brood of adults a year.

> **Second brood** The second generation of a multi-brooded species. Many of our Blue butterflies produce two broods a year, such as the Holly Blue.

> **Double brood** Or 'double brooded'. A butterfly species that produces two broods or generations a year.

Chrysalid/chrysalis Alternative words for pupa and pupae.

Cocoon Protective silk casing within which many moths pupate.

Dispersal stage Butterflies fly, caterpillars just crawl. The butterfly is therefore the main life stage in which the species can spread in search of new habitats.

Hibernaculum A tiny leaf tent in which the larvae of a few of our butterflies spend the winter, notably the White Admiral.

Larva/larvae/larval The technical words for caterpillar, caterpillars and the caterpillar (or larval) stage.

Pupa/pupae/pupal Often called the chrysalis stage, and confused with the word cocoon. The pupal stage is the development stage between the caterpillar and the adult butterfly. Caterpillars, or larvae, form a pupa – or pupate – and go into the pupal stage. None of the pupating larvae of our butterflies construct proper cocoons (like the silk moths), though a few of the Browns and Blues spin a few loose threads.

Pupate The process of turning from a caterpillar or larva into a pupa or chrysalis is called pupation – it's when the larvae pupate.

Further Reading

Eeles, P. *Life Cycles of British & Irish Butterflies.*
(Pisces Publications, Newbury, Berks, 2019)

Thomas, J.A. & Lewington, R. *The Butterflies of
Britain and Ireland*, third edition. (British Wildlife
Publishing, Oxford, 2014)

Waring, P., Townsend, M. & Lewington, R. *Field Guide
to the Moths of Great Britain and Ireland*, third edition.
(Bloomsbury Natural History, London, 2018)

butterfly-conservation.org – The website of Butterfly
Conservation, a charity dedicated to the conservation
of butterflies, moths and their habitats in the UK.

ukbutterflies.co.uk – A website for UK butterfly
enthusiasts.

Index